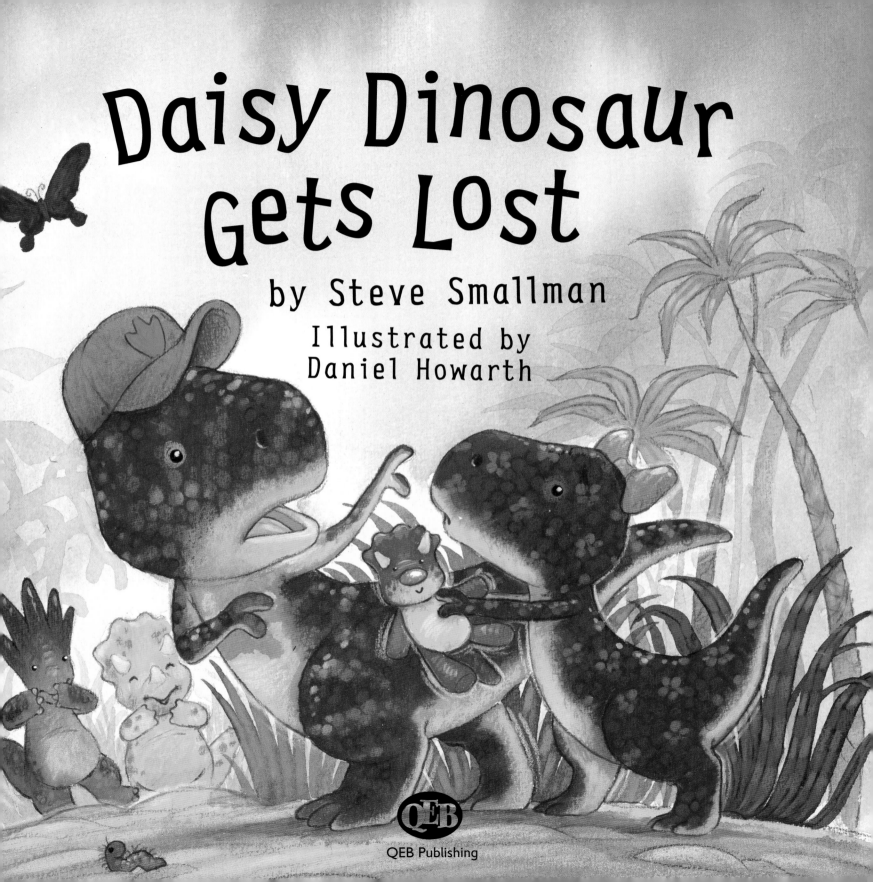

Daisy Dinosaur Gets Lost

by Steve Smallman

Illustrated by Daniel Howarth

QEB Publishing

"See you later!" said Rex.

"Not so fast," said Mom. "I want you to take your sister."

"But Mom!" groaned Rex. "She's too little to come to the swamp!"

"No buts, Rex. Daisy, be good and do what Rex tells you to do," said Mom.

"Come on, Wex!" said Daisy, and off they went.

Tubs and Spike were waiting at the swamp.

"Oooooooh, look!" they laughed.
"Rex is holding hands with a girl!"

Rex's face turned red.

"Let go of my hand!" he growled.
And Daisy did as she was told.

"She did what you said. Tell her to stand on one leg!" cried Tubs.

Rex was so annoyed that he told Daisy to stand on one leg.

And Daisy did as she was told.

"This is fun!" said Spike.

"Tell her to make a face."

"Tell her to hop on the spot."

"Tell her to throw her toy in the air."

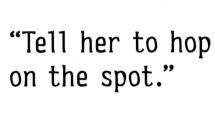

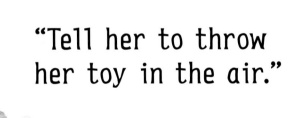

And Daisy did as she was told.

"This is boring," said Rex. "Let's climb trees!"
Daisy couldn't even reach the lowest branch.

"Wex," she called. "Hup me, Wex!"

"Hup me, too, Wexy-woo!" laughed Spike.

"Just stay there, Daisy!"
shouted Rex angrily.

And Daisy did as
she was told.

Then the boys played soccer.

"Can I play, Wex?" asked Daisy.

"Yes," said Rex, "and Bogbog can play, too."

"Weally?" said Daisy with a big smile.

"Yes, you can be the goalposts."

Spike aimed for the goal, and WHACK!
It hit the post.

"Bogbog!" cried Daisy, and ran to pick
him up, just as Rex was about to score.

Rex was angry. So was Daisy.

"Wex, kiss Bogbog better!" she cried.

"GET LOST, DAISY!" he shouted.

Rex stomped off, red-faced, to throw stones into a nearby pond.

Spike and Tubs joined in, and soon they were having a great time.

"Come and throw some ploppers, Daisy," called Rex.

But she wasn't there.

"Where's Daisy?" asked Rex.

Rex saw a little trail of footprints heading off deeper into the swamp and followed them.

He searched high and low, but he couldn't find her anywhere. Then he heard a noise ...

It was Daisy, sitting underneath some tangled tree roots.

"What are you doing, Daisy?" asked Rex gently.

"Getting lost," she cried.
"Like you told me to."

"I'm sorry, Daisy," said Rex.
"I didn't mean it."

Daisy cheered up.

"Will you play with me now?" asked Daisy.

"Yes," said Rex, smiling.

"And give me a
stompasauwus wide?"

"Yes."

"And throw ploppers?"

"Yes!"

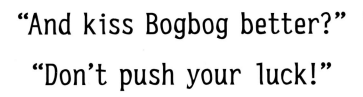

"And kiss Bogbog better?"

"Don't push your luck!"

Notes for Parents and Teachers

- Look at the front cover of the book together. Can the children guess what the story might be about? Read the title together. Does that give them a clue?

- When the children have read the story, or after you have read it to them, ask them which character, Daisy or Rex, was most like them. Did they feel more sympathy for Rex, whose day at the swamp was ruined, or Daisy, whose big brother wouldn't play with her?

- Why didn't Rex want to take his little sister to the swamp? Would he have minded so much if Spike and Tubs hadn't been there, too? What would the children have done in the same situation? Would it have been any different if Rex had had a little brother instead?

- Rex and his friends played lots of games together. Ask the children what their favorite games are. Discuss which games are fun for everyone to play, whether you are big or little, a boy or a girl.

- What does Rex really feel about his sister? How do the children feel about their siblings? If they don't have any, ask them what they think would be good or bad about having a brother or sister.

- Ask the children to draw a picture of their brother, their sister, or themselves as a dinosaur!

Copyright © QEB Publishing, Inc. 2010

Published in the United States by
QEB Publishing, Inc.
3 Wrigley, Suite A
Irvine, CA 92618

ISBN 978 1 60992 062 3

Printed in China

Editor: Amanda Askew
Designers: Vida and Luke Kelly

A CIP record for this book is available from the Library of Congress.